Mere Christianity
Journal

Mere Christianity
Journal

———— • ————

C. S. Lewis

HarperSanFrancisco
A Division of HarperCollinsPublishers

inspirio™

HarperCollins books may be purchased for educational, business, or sales promotional use. For information please write: Special Markets Department, Harper-Collins Publishers, Inc., 10 East 53rd Street, New York, NY 10022.

HarperCollins Web site: http://www.harpercollins.com
Inspirio, the gift group of Zondervan, www.inspiriogifts.com
HarperCollins®, ✦®, and HarperSanFrancisco™ are
trademarks of HarperCollins Publishers, Inc.

Compiler: Molly Detweiler
Project Manager: Thomas P. Dean
FIRST EDITION
Designed by Joseph Rutt

Printed in China

Library of Congress Cataloging-in-Publication Data is available upon request.
ISBN 0–06–072765–9
04 05 06 07 08 HK 10 9 8 7 6 5 4 3 2 1

Contents

Right and Wrong as a Clue to the Meaning of the Universe

CHAPTER ONE

The Law of Human Nature

*N*owadays, when we talk of the 'laws of nature' we usually mean things like gravitation, or heredity, or the laws of chemistry. But when older thinkers called the Law of Right and Wrong 'the law of Nature', they really meant the Law of Human Nature. The idea was that, just as all bodies are governed by the law of gravitation, and organisms by biological laws, so the creature called man also had his law—with this great difference, that a body could not choose whether it obeyed the law of gravitation or not, but a man could choose either to obey the Law of Human Nature or to disobey it. —C S L

In what ways does the Law of Human Nature work in your life?
Where does your knowledge of this law come from?

_____

_____

_____

_____

_____

_____

_____

> This is the quality peculiar to man, wherein he differs from other animals, that he alone is endowed with perception to distinguish right from wrong, justice from injustice.
> ARISTOTLE

_____

_____

_____

*T*hink of a country where people were admired for running away in battle, or where a man felt proud of double-crossing all the people who had been kindest to him. You might just as well try to imagine a country where two and two made five. —c s l

What laws of right and wrong govern your life? Why do you follow these rules? How did you come to believe these laws were right and that going against them was wrong?

Right is right, even if
everyone is against it; and
wrong is wrong, even if
everyone is for it.
WILLIAM PENN

*T*hese, then, are the two points I wanted to make. First, that human beings, all over the earth, have this curious idea that they ought to behave in a certain way, and cannot really get rid of it. Secondly, that they do not in fact behave in that way. They know the Law of Nature; they break it. These two facts are the foundation of all clear thinking about ourselves and the universe we live in. —c s l

Do you agree with Lewis's statement? What real world examples prove or disprove this idea for you?

> Good people do not
> need laws to tell them to
> act responsibly, while
> bad people will find a
> way around the laws.
>
> PLATO

CHAPTER TWO

Some Objections

We all know what it feels like to be prompted by instinct—by mother love, or sexual instinct, or the instinct for food. It means that you feel a strong want or desire to act in a certain way. And, of course, we sometimes do feel just that sort of desire to help another person: and no doubt that desire is due to the herd instinct. But feeling a desire to help is quite different from feeling that you ought to help whether you want to or not. —C S L

Describe a time when you countered "a natural instinct" because you thought it was the right thing to do something else instead. How did you make this decision? What does this say about how the idea of a universal Moral Law works in our lives?

_____

_____

_____

_____

_____

_____

_____

_____

_____

_____

_____

_____

_____

We ought to do good to
others as simply and as
naturally as a horse runs, or
a bee makes honey, or a vine
bears grapes season after
season without thinking of
the grapes it has borne.
MARCUS AURELIUS

*T*he most dangerous thing you can do is to take any one impulse of your own nature and set it up as the thing you ought to follow at all costs. There is not one of them which will not make us into devils if we set it up as an absolute guide. You might think love of humanity in general was safe, but it is not. If you leave out justice you will find yourself breaking agreements and faking evidence in trials 'for the sake of humanity', and become in the end a cruel and treacherous man. —C S L

What experiences have you had of people or movements that take a "good" thing and go too far with it? Have you ever found yourself in the uncomfortable position of being in the wrong despite having noble intentions? Why does Lewis call "dangerous" the tendency to make one impulse absolute?

There is a way that seems
   right to a man,
but in the end it leads to death.
        PROVERBS 14:12 NIV

CHAPTER THREE

The Reality of the Law

The laws of nature, as applied to stones or trees, may only mean 'what Nature, in fact, does'. But if you turn to the Law of Human Nature, the Law of Decent Behaviour, it is a different matter. That law certainly does not mean 'what human beings, in fact, do'; for as I said before, many of them do not obey this law at all, and none of them obey it completely. The law of gravity tells you what stones do if you drop them; but the Law of Human Nature tells you what human beings ought to do and do not. —CSL

What makes the Law of Human Nature a "law" when it is not always followed? What examples can you cite that show that this law is universally recognized? How have you encountered this "Law of Human Nature"?

Man is the only animal
that laughs and weeps, for
he is the only animal that
is struck with the
difference between what
things are, and what they
ought to be.
WILLIAM HAZLITT

*H*uman beings, after all, have some sense; they see that you cannot have any real safety or happiness except in a society where every one plays fair, and it is because they see this that they try to behave decently. Now, of course, it is perfectly true that safety and happiness can only come from individuals, classes, and nations being honest and fair and kind to each other. It is one of the most important truths in the world. But as an explanation of why we feel as we do about Right and Wrong it just misses the point. If we ask: 'Why ought I to be unselfish?' and you reply 'Because it is good for society', we may then ask, 'Why should I care what's good for society except when it happens to pay *me* personally?' and then you will have to say, 'Because you ought to be unselfish'—which simply brings us back to where we started. —c s l

Lewis is arguing that our instinct to be unselfish comes from a "law" everyone somehow just "knows." Examine your own story and try to identify the ways you came to know about this impulse to act unselfishly toward others. How did you learn that being unselfish is the right thing to do?

The highest morality, if
not inspired and vitalized
by religion, is but as the
marble statue, or the
silent corpse, to the living
and perfect man.
SAMUEL I. PRIME

The Moral Law, or Law of Human Nature, is not simply a fact about human behaviour in the same way as the Law of Gravitation is, or may be, simply a fact about how heavy objects behave. On the other hand, it is not a mere fancy, for we cannot get rid of the idea, and most of the things we say and think about men would be reduced to nonsense if we did. And it is not simply a statement about how we should like men to behave for our own convenience; for the behaviour we call bad or unfair is not exactly the same as the behaviour we find inconvenient, and may even be the opposite. Consequently, this Rule of Right and Wrong, or Law of Human Nature, or whatever you call it, must somehow or other be a real thing—a thing that is really there, not made up by ourselves. And yet it is not a fact in the ordinary sense, in the same way as our actual behaviour is a fact. It begins to look as if we shall have to admit that there is more than one kind of reality; that, in this particular case, there is something above and beyond the ordinary facts of men's behaviour, and yet quite definitely real—a real law, which none of us made, but which we find pressing on us. —C S L

What does it mean that there is another reality than the world of "facts"—a reality from which we get our ideas of right and wrong? What do you think Lewis means by saying the "Law of Human Nature" is "real" but "not a fact in the ordinary sense"?

> All sects are different, because
> they come from men; morality
> is everywhere the same,
> because it comes from God.
> VOLTAIRE

CHAPTER FOUR

What Lies Behind the Law

We want to know whether the universe simply happens to be what it is for no reason or whether there is a power behind it that makes it what it is. Since that power, if it exists, would be not one of the observed facts but a reality which makes them, no mere observation of the facts can find it. There is only one case in which we can know whether there is anything more, namely our own case. And in that one case we find there is. Or put it the other way round. If there was a controlling power outside the universe, it could not show itself to us as one of the facts inside the universe—no more than the architect of a house could actually be a wall or staircase or fireplace in that house. The only way in which we could expect it to show itself would be inside ourselves as an influence or command trying to get us to behave in a certain way. —C S L

Describe a time when you felt that a power outside of yourself was guiding you. How did you sense it? According to Lewis, why couldn't God reveal his intentions for us in a more direct manner?

_____

_____

_____

_____

_____

_____

_____

_____

_____

A revelation is not made for the purpose of showing to indolent men that which, by faculties already given to them, they may show to themselves; no: but for the purpose of showing that which the moral darkness of man will not, without supernatural light, allow him to perceive.

THOMAS DE QUINCEY

CHAPTER FIVE

We Have Cause to Be Uneasy

We all want progress. But progress means getting nearer to the place where you want to be. And if you have taken a wrong turning, then to go forward does not get you any nearer. If you are on the wrong road, progress means doing an about-turn and walking back to the right road; and in that case the man who turns back soonest is the most progressive man. We have all seen this when doing arithmetic. When I have started a sum the wrong way, the sooner I admit this and go back and start again, the faster I shall get on. There is nothing progressive about being pig headed and refusing to admit a mistake. And I think if you look at the present state of the world, it is pretty plain that humanity has been making some big mistakes. We are on the wrong road. And if that is so, we must go back. Going back is the quickest way on. —CSL

Have you ever had to make an "about-turn" in your life? How easy was it to change course? Lewis is countering the notion that Christianity is somehow outdated or backward looking, versus being modern and progressive. Why do you think Christianity has this reputation?

> A man should never be ashamed to own he has been in the wrong, which is but saying, in other words, that he is wiser today than he was yesterday.
>
> JONATHAN SWIFT

You find out more about God from the Moral Law than from the universe in general just as you find out more about a man by listening to his conversation than by looking at a house he has built. —C S L

What specific things have you learned about God through observing the universe? What specific things have you learned about God through the Moral Law?

> No one will be declared
> righteous in God's sight by
> observing the law; rather,
> through the law we become
> conscious of sin.
>
> ROMANS 3:20 NIV

*F*or the trouble is that one part of you is on His side and really agrees with his disapproval of human greed and trickery and exploitation. You may want Him to make an exception in your own case, to let you off this one time; but you know at the bottom that unless the power behind the world really and unalterably detests that sort of behaviour, then He cannot be good. On the other hand, we know that if there does exist an absolute goodness it must hate most of what we do. This is the terrible fix we are in. If the universe is not governed by an absolute goodness, then all our efforts are in the long run hopeless. But if it is, then we are making ourselves enemies to that goodness every day, and are not in the least likely to do any better tomorrow, and so our case is hopeless again. We cannot do without it, and we cannot do with it. God is the only comfort; He is also the supreme terror: the thing we most need and the thing we most want to hide from. —C S L

Why must God be absolutely good and why might this bother us? Have you experienced this struggle between both longing for God and fearing God? Describe both what you long for in God and what you fear.

> The law was given, in order
> to convert a great into a
> little man—to show that you
> have no power of your own
> for righteousness; and might
> thus, poor, needy, and
> destitute, flee to grace.
>
> AUGUSTINE OF HIPPO

Study Group Questions for

BOOK ONE

Right and Wrong as a Clue to the Meaning of the Universe

1. What are your thoughts about Lewis's idea of the "Law of Human Nature"? What are some of the laws of right and wrong that seem to be built into mankind?

2. What would be the consequences of a country that lived by morals completely opposite from what we would call right and wrong, as Lewis suggests? How do those consequences serve as proof that there is an absolute right and wrong?

3. Why are humans the only creatures who choose whether or not to obey Natural Laws? What does this ability to choose say about humanity's place in the universe?

4. Why do you think that people choose to act against the Moral Law, even when they agree that it is the right way to live? (For example, people generally agree that it is always good to be honest, but no one tells all of the truth all of the time.)

5. What does the Moral Law reveal about the nature of the universe? What does the Moral Law reveal about the nature of God?

6. Is the universe governed by absolute goodness? If so, what is the human responsibility to that goodness? If not, what does that mean about the nature of good and evil?

What Christians Believe

CHAPTER ONE

The Rival Conceptions of God

*I*f you are an atheist you do have to believe that the main point in
all the religions of the whole world is simply one huge mistake. If
you are a Christian, you are free to think that all those religions, even
the queerest ones, contain at least some hint of the truth. When I
was an atheist I had to try to persuade myself that most of the
human race have always been wrong about the question that mat-
tered to them most; when I became a Christian I was able to take a
more liberal view. But, of course, being a Christian does mean thinking that where Christianity differs from other religions, Christianity is
right and they are wrong. As in arithmetic—there is only one right
answer to a sum, and all other answers are wrong; but some of the
wrong answers are much nearer to being right than others. —C S L

*What truths, if any, have you encountered in the religions other
than the one you follow? Lewis compares the issue of which religion
is true to a problem of arithmetic: there can only be one right
answer. Do you agree with Lewis here? By what criteria would you
judge one religion to be true and another to be wrong or less
accurate?*

All truth, wherever it is
found, belongs to us as
Christians.
JUSTIN MARTYR

*P*antheists usually believe that God, so to speak, animates the universe as you animate your body: that the universe almost *is* God, so that if it did not exist He would not exist either, and anything you find in the universe is a part of God. The Christian idea is quite different. They think God invented and made the universe—like a man making a picture or composing a tune. A painter is not a picture, and he does not die if his picture is destroyed. You may say, 'He's put a lot of himself into it,' but you only mean that all its beauty and interest has come out of his head. His skill is not the picture in the same way that it is in his head, or even in his hands. —C S L

Do you believe God is in all things, animating all things, or that God is above all things and creator of all? Why do you believe the way you do? What difference do you think it makes to believe one versus the other?

> The world forgets you, its
> creator, and falls in love
> with what you have created
> instead of with you.
> AUGUSTINE OF HIPPO

CHAPTER TWO

The Invasion

*R*eality, in fact, is usually something you could not have guessed. That is one of the reasons I believe Christianity. It is a religion you could not have guessed. If it offered us just the kind of universe we had always expected, I should feel we were making it up. But, in fact, it is not the sort of thing anyone would have made up. It has just that queer twist about it that real things have. —C S L

Do you think there are more aspects of Christianity that have this quality of being different than anyone would have expected? Why would these be arguments for the truth of Christianity?

> Christianity is a scheme quite beyond our comprehension.
>
> JOSEPH BUTLER

You can be good for the mere sake of goodness: you cannot be bad for the mere sake of badness. You can do a kind action when you are not feeling kind and when it gives you no pleasure, simply because kindness is right; but no one ever did a cruel action simply because cruelty is wrong—only because cruelty was pleasant or useful to him. In other words badness cannot succeed even in being bad in the same way in which goodness is good. Goodness is, so to speak, itself: badness is only spoiled goodness. —C S L

Why can't someone be bad for badness sake? What do you think Lewis means by saying "badness is only goodness spoiled"? Think of instances where you have encountered people at their worst: How can this view of evil or badness as "goodness spoiled" be used in explaining those situations? How were these people misapplying some good thing?

This is a good universe. There is no permanent place in it for evil. Yea, it would seem as if God and man and the universe itself were opposed to evil. Evil may hide behind this fallacy and that, but it will be hunted from fallacy to fallacy until there is no more fallacy for it to hide behind.

THOMAS CARLYLE

*E*nemy-occupied territory—that is what this world is. Christianity is the story of how the rightful king has landed, you might say landed in disguise, and is calling us all to take part in a great campaign of sabotage. When you go to church you are really listening-in to the secret wireless from our friends: that is why the enemy is so anxious to prevent us from going. —C S L

Does the idea of the world as "enemy-occupied territory" change your perspective of Christianity? What parallels can you draw between what you know of war and living the Christian life?

_____

_____

_____

_____

_____

_____

_____

_____

_____

_____

_____

_____

_____

_____

_____

> The devil does not sleep, nor is the flesh yet dead; therefore, you must never cease your preparation for battle, because on the right and on the left are enemies who never rest.
>
> THOMAS À KEMPIS

CHAPTER THREE

The Shocking Alternative

God created things which had free will. That means creatures which can go either wrong or right. Some people think they can imagine a creature which was free but had no possibility of going wrong; I cannot. If a thing is free to be good it is also free to be bad. And free will is what has made evil possible. Why, then, did God give them free will? Because free will, though it makes evil possible, is also the only thing that makes possible any love or goodness or joy worth having. —CSL

Why is having free will the only way for making love, goodness, and joy worth having? How does it change how you see your life knowing God wants you to do right and to love him but that he gave you the free choice to choose to do wrong and to ignore him?

God, having placed good
and evil in our power, has
given us full freedom of
choice; he does not keep
back the unwilling, but
embraces the willing.

JOHN CHRYSOSTOM

Now God designed the human machine to run on Himself. He Himself is the fuel our spirits were designed to burn, or the food our spirits were designed to feed on. There is no other. That is why it is just no good asking God to make us happy in our own way without bothering about religion. God cannot give us a happiness and peace apart from Himself, because it is not there. There is no such thing.
—CSL

In observing the nature of the world today do you see proof of Lewis's argument that happiness is only found in God? Where have you found true happiness and peace?

_____

_____

_____

_____

_____

_____

_____

_____

_____

_____

_____

_____

_____

_____

_____

_____

_____

_____

_____

> If man is not made for God, why is he happy only in God?
>
> BLAISE PASCAL

I am trying here to prevent anyone saying the really foolish thing that people often say about Him: 'I'm ready to accept Jesus as a great moral teacher, but I don't accept His claim to be God.' That is the one thing we must not say. A man who was merely a man and said the sort of things Jesus said would not be a great moral teacher. He would either be a lunatic—on a level with the man who says he is a poached egg—or else he would be the Devil of Hell. You must make your choice. Either this man was, and is, the Son of God: or else a madman or something worse. You can shut Him up for a fool, you can spit at Him and kill Him as a demon; or you can fall at His feet and call Him Lord and God. But let us not come with any patronising nonsense about His being a great human teacher. He has not left that open to us. He did not intend to. —C S L

What are the claims Jesus made that make it "foolish" to say that he was just "a great moral teacher"? If what Lewis says is true, why do so many people deny Jesus' deity but still admire him as a teacher or a really good man?

I know men; and I tell you that Jesus Christ is no mere man. Between him and every other person in the world there is no possible term of comparison.

NAPOLEON BONAPARTE

CHAPTER FOUR

The Perfect Penitent

We believe that the death of Christ is just that point in history at which something absolutely unimaginable from outside shows through into our own world. And if we cannot picture even the atoms of which our own world is built, of course we are not going to be able to picture this. Indeed, if we found that we could fully understand it, that very fact would show it was not what it professes to be—the inconceivable, the uncreated, the thing from beyond nature, striking down into nature like lightning. —C S L

How can we commit our lives to something that is impossible for us to comprehend? How does its incomprehensibility make it more credible?

If I might comprehend Jesus
Christ, I could not believe in
Him. He would be no greater
than myself. Such is my
consciousness of sin and
inability that I must have a
superhuman Savior.

DANIEL WEBSTER

When you teach a child writing, you hold its hand while it forms the letters: that is, it forms the letters because you are forming them. We love and reason because God loves and reasons and holds our hand while we do it. Now if we had not fallen, that would be all plain sailing. But unfortunately we now need God's help in order to do something which God, in His own nature, never does at all—to surrender, to suffer, to submit, to die. Nothing in God's nature corresponds to this process at all. So that the one road for which we now need God's leadership most of all is a road God, in His own nature, has never walked. God can share only what He has: this thing, in His own nature, He has not.

But supposing God became a man—suppose our human nature which can suffer and die was amalgamated with God's nature in one person—then that person could help us. He could surrender His will, and suffer and die, because He was man; and He could do it perfectly because He was God. —c s l

Why would God become a man if it meant he had to suffer and die? Why didn't he simply allow us to do it on our own?

_____

_____

_____

_____

_____

_____

_____

_____

_____

_____

> God clothed himself in vile
> man's flesh so He might be
> weak enough to suffer woe.
>
> JOHN DONNE

CHAPTER FIVE

The Practical Conclusion

*T*he perfect surrender and humiliation were undergone by Christ: perfect because He was God, surrender and humiliation because He was man. Now the Christian belief is that if we somehow share the humility and suffering of Christ we shall also share in His conquest of death and find a new life after we have died and in it become perfect, and perfectly happy, creatures. This means something much more than our trying to follow His teaching. People often ask when the next step in evolution—the step to something beyond man—will happen. But in the Christian view, it has happened already. In Christ a new kind of man appeared: and the new kind of life which began in Him is to be put into us. —c s l

How do you "share in the humility and suffering of Christ"? Have you experienced this new kind of life?

_____

_____

_____

_____

_____

_____

_____

_____

_____

_____

_____

_____

_____

Therefore, if anyone is in Christ,
he is a new creation; the old has
gone, the new has come!
2 CORINTHIANS 5:17 NIV

Your natural life is derived from your parents; that does not mean it will stay there if you do nothing about it. You can lose it by neglect, or you can drive it away by committing suicide. You have to feed it and look after it: but always remember you are not making it, you are only keeping up a life you got from someone else. In the same way a Christian can lose the Christ-life which has been put into him, and he has to make efforts to keep it. But even the best Christian that ever lived is not acting on his own steam—he is only nourishing or protecting a life he could never have acquired by his own efforts.
—CSL

What do you do to nourish your spiritual life? Have there been times when you felt your spiritual life was undernourished or even at risk?

> As the apple is not the cause
> of the apple tree, but a fruit of
> it: even so good works are not
> the cause of our salvation, but
> a sign and a fruit of the same.
> DANIEL CAWDRAY

When the author walks on to the stage the play is over. God is going to invade, all right: but what is the good of saying you are on His side then, when you see the whole natural universe melting away like a dream and something else—something it never entered your head to conceive—comes crashing in; something so beautiful to some of us and so terrible to others that none of us will have any choice left? For this time it will be God without disguise; something so overwhelming that it will strike either irresistible love or irresistible horror into every creature. It will be too late then to choose your side. There is no use saying you choose to lie down when it has become impossible to stand up. That will not be the time for choosing: it will be the time when we discover which side we really have chosen, whether we realised it before or not. Now, today, this moment, is our chance to choose the right side. God is holding back to give us that chance. It will not last for ever. We must take it or leave it. —C S L

Do you feel God has asked you to choose a side? Why can't we wait for the "proof" before we choose sides?

> Time is short. Eternity is
> long. It is only reasonable
> that this short life be lived
> in the light of eternity.
> C. H. SPURGEON

Study Group Questions for

BOOK TWO

What Christians Believe

1. Does it take more faith to believe that the whole human race is wrong about the existence of God or to actually believe that God exists?

2. What do you think of Lewis's statement that all religions contain elements of the truth, but that Christianity *is* the truth?

3. If God is in everything (as in pantheism) and he only exists because the universe exists, is he really God? Why or why not?

4. How is reality "something you could not have guessed"? What facts about the "real world" are unlike anything you could have imagined on your own? What does that say about the existence of God?

5. Discuss the idea that you "can be good for the mere sake of goodness: you cannot be bad for the mere sake of badness." What are some concrete examples of this principle?

6. Why would God create creatures with free will if he knew that meant that they could choose evil? What does this fact reveal about the nature of God?

7. Is true joy only found in God?

8. Many people say they respect Jesus as a prophet or a good teacher, but do not believe that he is God. Lewis asserts that this is not possible—Jesus is either God or a madman or demon. What do you think?

9. Discuss the idea of the "perfect penitent"—God becoming man so he could know suffering and death, and in turn help us to die to ourselves. How does this bring new life to humanity? What does this reveal to us about God?

10. Why must we "choose sides" now—either accepting or rejecting God? Why isn't living a "good life" enough to give us a meaningful existence?

BOOK THREE

Christian Behaviour

CHAPTER ONE

The Three Parts of Morality

There are two ways in which the human machine goes wrong. One is when human individuals drift apart from one another, or else collide with one another and do one another damage, by cheating or bullying. The other is when things go wrong inside the individual—when the different parts of him (his different faculties and desires and so on) either drift apart or interfere with one another. You can get the idea plain if you think of us as a fleet of ships sailing in formation. The voyage will be a success only, in the first place, if the ships do not collide and get in one another's way; and secondly, if each ship is seaworthy and has her engines in good order. As a matter of fact, you cannot have either of these two things without the other. If the ships keep on having collisions they will not remain seaworthy very long. On the other hand, if their steering gears are out of order they will not be able to avoid collisions. Or, if you like, think of humanity as a band playing a tune. To get a good result, you need two things. Each player's individual instrument must be in tune and also each must come in at the right moment so as to combine with all the others.

But there is one thing we have not yet taken into account. We have not asked where the fleet is trying to get to, or what piece of music the band is trying to play. The instruments might all be in tune and might all come in at the right moment, but even so the performance would not be a success if they had been engaged to provide dance music and actually played nothing but Dead Marches. And however well the fleet sailed, its voyage would be a failure if it were meant to reach New York and actually arrived at Calcutta.

Morality, then, seems to be concerned with three things. Firstly, with fair play and harmony between individuals. Secondly, with what might be called tidying up or harmonising the things inside each individual. Thirdly, with the general purpose of human life as a whole: what man was made for: what course the whole fleet ought to be on: what tune the conductor of the band wants it to play. —C S L

What is the importance of each part of morality as Lewis describes them here? If we are moral within ourselves and with others, why would it matter what the overall purpose of morality is to human life as a whole?

The only morality that is clear in its course, pure in its precepts, and efficacious in its influence, is the morality of the gospel. All else, at last, is but idolatry—the worship of something of man's own creation, and that, imperfect and feeble like himself, and wholly insufficient to give him support and strength.

JOHN SARGEANT

CHAPTER TWO

The 'Cardinal Virtues'

*P*rudence means practical common sense, taking the trouble to think out what you are doing and what is likely to come of it. Nowadays most people hardly think of Prudence as one of the 'virtues'. In fact, because Christ said we could only get into His world by being like children, many Christians have the idea that, provided you are 'good', it does not matter being a fool. But that is a misunderstanding. In the first place, most children show plenty of 'prudence' about doing the things that they are really interested in, and think them out quite sensibly. In the second place, as St Paul points out, Christ never meant that we were to remain children in *intelligence*: on the contrary. He told us to be not only 'as harmless as doves', but also 'as wise as serpents'. He wants a child's heart, but a grown-up's head. —c s l

What are some "real world" examples of acting prudently? Why is being prudent considered a "cardinal virtue"?

_____

_____

_____

_____

| Prudence is right reason in action. |
| THOMAS AQUINAS |

_____

_____

_____

_____

*T*emperance is, unfortunately, one of those words that has changed its meaning. It now usually means teetotalism. But in the days when the second Cardinal virtue was christened 'Temperance', it meant nothing of the sort. Temperance referred not specially to drink, but to all pleasures; and it meant not abstaining, but going the right length and no further. —C S L

What does it mean to be temperate? Is this considered to be a virtue in today's world?

> Temperate temperance is best; intemperate temperance injures the cause of temperance.
> MARTIN LUTHER

*J*ustice means much more than the sort of thing that goes on in law courts. It is the old name for everything we should now call 'fairness'; it includes honesty, give and take, truthfulness, keeping promises, and all that side of life. And Fortitude includes both kinds of courage— the kind that faces danger as well as the kind that 'sticks it' under pain. 'Guts' is perhaps the nearest modern English. You will notice, of course, that you cannot practise any of the other virtues very long without bringing this one into play. —C S L

When have you faced injustice? What did you do in the face of unfairness? How does Lewis's idea of "justice" contrast with a legal sense? What role does fortitude play when practicing other virtues? Why is it a virtue to face danger or to have "guts"?

I cannot praise a fugitive and cloistered virtue, unexercised and unbreathed, that never sallies out and sees her adversary, but slinks out of the race, where that immortal garland is to be run for, not without dust and heat.

JOHN MILTON

CHAPTER THREE

Social Morality

*T*he first thing to get clear about Christian morality between man and man is that in this department Christ did not come to preach any brand new morality. The Golden Rule of the New Testament (Do as you would be done by) is a summing up of what every one, at bottom, had always known to be right. —c s l

---

Why do we know that the Golden Rule is right? In what ways do we see the Golden Rule at work?

_____

_____

_____

_____

_____

_____

_____

_____

_____

Sometime when you have a few spare moments, try to think of some other basic principle that would cure all the world's ills faster than the Golden Rule put into practice.
FRIENDLY ADVENTURER

_____

_____

_____

_____

*T*he second thing to get clear is that Christianity has not, and does not profess to have, a detailed political programme for applying 'Do as you would be done by' to a particular society at a particular moment. It could not have. It is meant for all men at all times and the particular programme which suited one place or time would not suit another. And, anyhow, that is not how Christianity works. When it tells you to feed the hungry it does not give you lessons in cookery. When it tells you to read the Scriptures it does not give you lessons in Hebrew and Greek, or even in English grammar. It was never intended to replace or supersede the ordinary human arts and sciences: it is rather a director which will set them all to the right jobs, and a source of energy which will give them all new life, if only they will put themselves at its disposal. —c s l

What is our responsibility in light of the fact that Christianity tells us what we should do, but not how to do it?

_____

_____

_____

_____

_____

_____

_____

_____

_____

_____

_____

_____

_____

_____

> He who shall introduce into
> public affairs the principles of
> primitive Christianity will
> change the face of the world.
> BENJAMIN FRANKLIN

Charity—giving to the poor—is an essential part of Christian morality: in the frightening parable of the sheep and the goats it seems to be the point on which everything turns. Some people nowadays say that charity ought to be unnecessary and that instead of giving to the poor we ought to be producing a society in which there are no poor to give to. They may be quite right in saying that we ought to produce this kind of society. But if anyone thinks that, as a consequence, you can stop giving in the meantime, then he has parted company with all Christian morality. I do not believe one can settle how much we ought to give. I am afraid the only safe rule is to give more than we can spare. —C S L

What does Lewis mean when he says that the only "safe rule is to give more than we can spare"? Why is giving in this way "an essential part of Christian morality"?

As the purse is emptied,
the heart is filled.
VICTOR HUGO

CHAPTER FOUR

Morality and Psychoanalysis

When a man makes a moral choice two things are involved. One is the act of choosing. The other is the various feelings, impulses and so on which his psychological outfit presents him with, and which are the raw material of his choice. Now this raw material may be of two kinds. Either it may be what we would call normal: it may consist of the sort of feelings that are common to all men. Or else it may consist of quite unnatural feelings due to things that have gone wrong in his subconscious. Thus fear of things that are really dangerous would be an example of the first kind: an irrational fear of cats or spiders would be an example of the second kind. The desire of a man for a woman would be of the first kind: the perverted desire of a man for a man would be the second. Now what psychoanalysis undertakes to do is to remove the abnormal feelings, that is, to give the man better raw material for his acts of choice; morality is concerned with the acts of choice themselves. —C S L

What things in your personality and background affect your decision making every day? How does our psychological makeup influence how we make moral choices?

_____

_____

_____

_____

_____

_____

_____

The mind is the atmosphere
of the soul.
JOSEPH JOUBERT

However much you improve the man's raw material, you have still got something else: the real, free choice of the man, on the material presented to him, either to put his own advantage first or to put it last. And this free choice is the only thing that morality is concerned with.

The bad psychological material is not a sin but a disease. It does not need to be repented of, but to be cured. And by the way, that is very important. Human beings judge one another by their external actions. God judges them by their moral choices. —C S L

What difference does it make that God judges people by their choices and not their "psychological material"? Why doesn't he judge us on the basis of both these considerations?

Judge nothing before the
appointed time; wait till the Lord
comes. He will bring to light what
is hidden in darkness and will
expose the motives of men's hearts.

1 CORINTHIANS 4:5 NIV

Some of us who seem quite nice people may, in fact, have made so little use of a good heredity and a good upbringing that we are really worse than those whom we regard as fiends. Can we be quite certain how we should have behaved if we had been saddled with the psychological outfit, and then with the bad upbringing, and then with the power, say, of Himmler? That is why Christians are told not to judge. We see only the results which a man's choices make out of his raw material. But God does not judge him on the raw material at all, but on what he has done with it. Most of the man's psychological makeup is probably due to his body: when his body dies all that will fall off him, and the real central man, the thing that chose, that made the best or the worst out of this material, will stand naked. All sorts of nice things which we thought our own, but which were really due to a good digestion, will fall off some of us: all sorts of nasty things which were due to complexes or bad health will fall off others. We shall then, for the first time, see every one as he really was. There will be surprises. —C S L

What role does heredity and our upbringing play in how God sees us? In this light, how do you think God sees you?

When I get to heaven, I shall see three
wonders there. The first wonder will be
to see many there whom I did not expect
to see; the second wonder will be to miss
many people who I did expect to see; the
third and greatest of all will be to find
myself there.

JOHN NEWTON

CHAPTER FIVE

Sexual Morality

*I*n the first place our warped natures, the devils who tempt us, and all the contemporary propaganda for lust, combine to make us feel that the desires we are resisting are so 'natural', so 'healthy', and so reasonable, that it is almost perverse and abnormal to resist them. Poster after poster, film after film, novel after novel, associate the idea of sexual indulgence with the ideas of health, normality, youth, frankness, and good humour. Now this association is a lie. Like all powerful lies, it is based on a truth—the truth, acknowledged above, that sex in itself (apart from the excesses and obsessions that have grown round it) is 'normal' and 'healthy', and all the rest of it. The lie consists in the suggestion that any sexual act to which you are tempted at the moment is also healthy and normal. Now this, on any conceivable view, and quite apart from Christianity, must be nonsense. Surrender to all our desires obviously leads to impotence, disease, jealousies, lies, concealment, and everything that is the reverse of health, good humour, and frankness. For any happiness, even in this world, quite a lot of restraint is going to be necessary; so the claim made by every desire, when it is strong, to be healthy and reasonable, counts for nothing. —c s l

Why does chastity and sexual restraint seem so difficult and unreasonable to most people? What is the big lie Lewis describes? How have you seen this message expressed in our culture?

> There has never been,
> and cannot be, a good
> life, without self-control.
> LEO TOLSTOY

*I*n the second place, many people are deterred from seriously at-
tempting Christian chastity because they think (before trying) that it
is impossible. But when a thing has to be attempted, one must never
think about possibility or impossibility. Faced with an optional question in an examination paper, one considers whether one can do it or
not: faced with a compulsory question, one must do the best one
can. You may get some marks for a very imperfect answer: you will
certainly get none for leaving the question alone. Not only in exami-
nations but in war, in mountain climbing, in learning to skate, or
swim, or ride a bicycle, even in fastening a stiff collar with cold fin-
gers, people quite often do what seemed impossible before they did
it. It is wonderful what you can do when you have to. —C S L

*Why is Christian chastity considered impossible by some? What
things have you accomplished that at first seemed impossible? Why
did you even try? How did you succeed?*

_____

_____

_____

_____

_____

_____

_____

_____

_____

_____

_____

_____

We never test the
resources of God until we
attempt the impossible.

F. B. MEYER

CHAPTER SIX

Christian Marriage

*T*he Christian idea of marriage is based on Christ's words that a man and wife are to be regarded as a single organism—for that is what the words 'one flesh' would be in modern English. And the Christians believe that when He said this He was not expressing a sentiment but stating a fact—just as one is stating a fact when one says that a lock and its key are one mechanism, or that a violin and a bow are one musical instrument. The inventor of the human machine was telling us that its two halves, the male and the female, were made to be combined together in pairs, not simply on the sexual level, but totally combined. The monstrosity of sexual intercourse outside marriage is that those who indulge in it are trying to isolate one kind of union (the sexual) from all the other kinds of union which were intended to go along with it and make up the total union. —CSL

Do you agree with Lewis's idea of a husband and wife as one being, just as a violin and its bow are one instrument? Have you encountered a couple that seems to work in harmony this way?

There is nothing nobler or
more admirable than when two
people who see eye to eye keep
house as man and wife,
confounding their enemies and
delighting their friends.

HOMER

*T*he idea that 'being in love' is the only reason for remaining married really leaves no room for marriage as a contract or promise at all. If love is the whole thing, then the promise can add nothing; and if it adds nothing, then it should not be made. The curious thing is that lovers themselves, while they remain really in love, know this better than those who talk about love. As Chesterton pointed out, those who are in love have a natural inclination to bind themselves by promises. Love songs all over the world are full of vows of eternal constancy. The Christian law is not forcing upon the passion of love something which is foreign to that passion's own nature: it is demanding that lovers should take seriously something which their passion of itself impels them to do. —C S L

What reasons are there to remain in a marriage besides the feeling of "being in love"? What is the purpose behind making a promise to someone you love?

Two pure souls fused into one by an impassioned love—friends, counselors—a mutual support and inspiration to each other amid life's struggles, must know the highest human happiness; this is marriage; and this is the only cornerstone of an enduring home.

ELIZABETH CADY STANTON

*I*f the old fairy-tale ending 'They lived happily ever after' is taken to mean 'They felt for the next fifty years exactly as they felt the day before they were married', then it says what probably never was nor ever would be true, and would be highly undesirable if it were. Who could bear to live in that excitement for even five years? What would become of your work, your appetite, your sleep, your friendships? But, of course, ceasing to be 'in love' need not mean ceasing to love. Love in this second sense—love as distinct from 'being in love'—is not merely a feeling. It is a deep unity, maintained by the will and deliberately strengthened by habit; reinforced by (in Christian marriages) the grace which both partners ask, and receive, from God. They can have this love for each other even at those moments when they do not like each other; as you love yourself even when you do not like yourself. They can retain this love even when each would easily, if they allowed themselves, be 'in love' with someone else. 'Being in love' first moved them to promise fidelity: this quieter love enables them to keep the promise. It is on this love that the engine of marriage is run: being in love was the explosion that started it. —C S L

How does Lewis's ideas contrast with what our culture sees as "true love"? What roles do "will" and "habit" play in love?

> Husband and wife must delight
> in the love and company, and
> lives of each other. When
> husband and wife take pleasure
> in each other, it unites them in
> duty, it helps them with ease to
> do their work, and bear their
> burdens; and is a major part of
> the comfort of marriage.
>
> RICHARD BAXTER

CHAPTER SEVEN

Forgiveness

*F*or a long time I used to think this a silly, straw-splitting distinction: how could you hate what a man did and not hate the man? But years later it occurred to me that there was one man to whom I had been doing this all my life—namely myself. However much I might dislike my own cowardice or conceit or greed, I went on loving myself. There had never been the slightest difficulty about it. In fact the very reason why I hated the things was that I loved the man. Just because I loved myself, I was sorry to find that I was the sort of man who did those things. Consequently, Christianity does not want us to reduce by one atom the hatred we feel for cruelty and treachery. We ought to hate them. Not one word of what we have said about them needs to be unsaid. But it does want us to hate them in the same way in which we hate things in ourselves: being sorry that the man should have done such things, and hoping, if it is anyway possible, that somehow, sometime, somewhere he can be cured and made human again. —C S L

If we love ourselves in spite of hating some of the things we do, why do we find it so hard to extend that same love to others? How do you imagine applying "hate the sin; love the sinner" to those you want to forgive?

> Love the sinner but
> hate the sin.
> AUGUSTINE OF HIPPO

I imagine somebody will say, 'Well, if one is allowed to condemn the enemy's acts, and punish him, and kill him, what difference is left between Christian morality and the ordinary view?' All the difference in the world. Remember, we Christians think man lives for ever. Therefore, what really matters is those little marks or twists on the central, inside part of the soul which are going to turn it, in the long run, into a heavenly or hellish creature. We may kill if necessary, but we must not hate and enjoy hating. We may punish if necessary, but we must not enjoy it. In other words, something inside us, the feeling of resentment, the feeling that wants to get one's own back, must be simply killed. I do not mean that anyone can decide this moment that he will never feel it any more. That is not how things happen. I mean that every time it bobs its head up, day after day, year after year, all our lives long, we must hit it on the head. It is hard work, but the attempt is not impossible. Even while we kill and punish we must try to feel about the enemy as we feel about ourselves—to wish that he were not bad, to hope that he may, in this world or another, be cured: in fact, to wish his good. This is what is meant in the Bible by loving him: wishing his good, not feeling fond of him nor saying he is nice when he is not. —C S L

Does Lewis's explanation of loving your enemies as "wishing them good" give you a better understanding of the biblical command to "love your enemies"? Think of the person you have the most difficulty forgiving; can you wish them well?

> Whatever a person may be
> like, we must still love
> them because we love God.
> JOHN CALVIN

The Great Sin

According to Christian teachers, the essential vice, the utmost evil, is Pride. Unchastity, anger, greed, drunkenness, and all that are mere fleabites in comparison: it was through Pride that the devil became the devil: Pride leads to every other vice: it is the complete anti-God state of mind.

Does this seem to you exaggerated? If so, think it over. I pointed out a moment ago that the more pride one had, the more one disliked pride in others. In fact, if you want to find out how proud you are the easiest way is to ask yourself, 'How much do I dislike it when other people snub me, or refuse to take any notice of me, or shove their oar in, or patronise me, or show off?' The point is that each person's pride is in competition with every one else's pride. —C S L

Ask yourself the question Lewis poses above. When do you feel competitive with others? Does pride play a role in these comparisons?

The more proud anyone is himself, the more impatient he becomes at the slightest instance of it in other people. And the less humility anyone has, the more he demands and is delighted with it in other people.

WILLIAM LAW

The Christians are right: it is Pride which has been the chief cause of misery in every nation and every family since the world began. Other vices may sometimes bring people together: you may find good fellowship and jokes and friendliness among drunken people or unchaste people. But pride always means enmity—it *is* enmity. And not only enmity between man and man, but enmity to God.

In God you come up against something which is in every respect immeasurably superior to yourself. Unless you know God as that—and therefore, know yourself as nothing in comparison—you do not know God at all. As long as you are proud you cannot know God. A proud man is always looking down on things and people: and, of course, as long as you are looking down, you cannot see something that is above you. —C S L

Reflect on how pride works in your life. How does it affect your relationships at work, with your family, and with God?

As long as a man's soul is lifted up with pride, he will never truly know anything about faith, and never come to live by faith.

C. H. SPURGEON

It is a terrible thing that the worst of all the vices can smuggle itself into the very centre of our religious life. But you can see why. The other, and less bad, vices come from the devil working on us through our animal nature. But this does not come through our animal nature at all. It comes direct from hell. It is purely spiritual: consequently it is far more subtle and deadly. For the same reason, Pride can often be used to beat down the simpler vices. Teachers, in fact, often appeal to a boy's Pride, or, as they call it, his self-respect, to make him behave decently: many a man has overcome cowardice, or lust, or ill-temper, by learning to think that they are beneath his dignity—that is, by Pride. The devil laughs. He is perfectly content to see you becoming chaste and brave and self-controlled provided, all the time, he is setting up in you the Dictatorship of Pride—just as he would be quite content to see your chilblains cured if he was allowed, in return, to give you cancer. For Pride is spiritual cancer: it eats up the very possibility of love, or contentment, or even common sense. —C S L

Why is pride a "purely spiritual" vice? In what ways does pride eat away at love, contentment, and common sense?

> What a strange device of the devil
> is here, to overthrow all Christian
> meekness and gentleness . . . under
> a cloak of high sanctity and zeal,
> and boldness for Christ! And it is
> a remarkable instance of the
> weakness of the human mind, and
> how much too cunning the devil
> is for us!
>
> JONATHAN EDWARDS

CHAPTER NINE

Charity

*T*he rule for all of us is perfectly simple. Do not waste time bothering whether you 'love' your neighbour; act as if you did. As soon as we do this we find one of the great secrets. When you are behaving as if you loved someone, you will presently come to love him. If you injure someone you dislike, you will find yourself disliking him more. If you do him a good turn, you will find yourself disliking him less. —C S L

———◆———

Why does Lewis think it doesn't matter whether you feel love for someone? Why would acting as if you loved someone bring about feelings of love?

Accustom yourself continually
to make many acts of love, for
they enkindle and melt the soul.
TERESA OF AVILA

On the whole, God's love for us is a much safer subject to think about than our love for Him. Nobody can always have devout feelings: and even if we could, feelings are not what God principally cares about. Christian Love, either towards God or towards man, is an affair of the will. If we are trying to do His will we are obeying the commandment, 'Thou shalt love the Lord thy God.' He will give us feelings of love if He pleases. We cannot create them for ourselves, and we must not demand them as a right. But the great thing to remember is that, though our feelings come and go, His love for us does not. It is not wearied by our sins, or our indifference; and, therefore, it is quite relentless in its determination that we shall be cured of those sins, at whatever cost to us, at whatever cost to Him. —C S L

Why is Christian love "an affair of the will"? What does it mean for your life to know that God's love doesn't come and go?

I love my God, but with no
    love of mine
For I have none to give;
I love Thee, Lord, but all that
    love is Thine,
For by Thy life I live.
I am as nothing, and rejoice to be
Emptied and lost and
    swallowed up in Thee.

MADAME GUYON

CHAPTER TEN

Hope

Aim at Heaven and you will get earth 'thrown in': aim at earth and you will get neither. It seems a strange rule, but something like it can be seen at work in other matters. Health is a great blessing, but the moment you make health one of your main, direct objects you start becoming a crank and imagining there is something wrong with you. You are only likely to get health provided you want other things more—food, games, work, fun, open air. In the same way, we shall never save civilisation as long as civilisation is our main object. We must learn to want something else even more. —c s l

Can you think of another example where aiming at earth gets you nothing? What do you think it means to "aim at heaven" and what would change if you did?

_____

_____

_____

_____

_____

_____

_____

_____

_____

_____

_____

He who thinks most of
heaven will do most for earth.
ANONYMOUS

*T*he Christian says, 'Creatures are not born with desires unless satisfaction for those desires exists. A baby feels hunger: well, there is such a thing as food. A duckling wants to swim: well, there is such a thing as water. Men feel sexual desire: well, there is such a thing as sex. If I find in myself a desire which no experience in this world can satisfy, the most probable explanation is that I was made for another world. If none of my earthly pleasures satisfy it, that does not prove that the universe is a fraud. Probably earthly pleasures were never meant to satisfy it, but only to arouse it, to suggest the real thing. If that is so, I must take care, on the one hand, never to despise, or be unthankful for, these earthly blessings, and on the other, never to mistake them for the something else of which they are only a kind of copy, or echo, or mirage. I must keep alive in myself the desire for my true country, which I shall not find till after death; I must never let it get snowed under or turned aside; I must make it the main object of my life to press on to that other country and to help others to do the same.'

What do you think about Lewis's idea that our unsatisfied desire means that we were "made for another world"? How have you experienced this? How does this, or how should this, affect our lives now?

There is a heaven, for ever,
day by day,
The upward longing of
my soul doth tell me so.

PAUL LAURENCE DUNBAR

CHAPTER ELEVEN

Faith

Now Faith, in the sense in which I am here using the word, is the art of holding on to things your reason has once accepted, in spite of your changing moods. For moods will change, whatever view your reason takes. I know that by experience. Now that I am a Christian I do have moods in which the whole thing looks very improbable: but when I was an atheist I had moods in which Christianity looked terribly probable. This rebellion of your moods against your real self is going to come anyway. That is why Faith is such a necessary virtue: unless you teach your moods 'where they get off', you can never be either a sound Christian or even a sound atheist, but just a creature dithering to and fro, with its beliefs really dependent on the weather and the state of its digestion. Consequently one must train the habit of Faith. —c s l

In what areas of your everyday life do you "teach your moods 'where they get off'"? What can you do now to start training the habits of your faith?

_____

_____

_____

_____

_____

_____

_____

> If God promises something, then faith must fight a long and bitter fight, for reason or the flesh judges that God's promises are impossible. Therefore faith must battle against reason and its doubts.
>
> MARTIN LUTHER

CHAPTER TWELVE

Faith

Now we cannot, in that sense, discover our failure to keep God's law except by trying our very hardest (and then failing). Unless we really try, whatever we say there will always be at the back of our minds the idea that if we try harder next time we shall succeed in being completely good. Thus, in one sense, the road back to God is a road of moral effort, of trying harder and harder. But in another sense it is not trying that is ever going to bring us home. All this trying leads up to the vital moment at which you turn to God and say, 'You must do this. I can't.'

If we know that no matter how hard we try to "be good" we will fail, why do we continue to try harder and harder? Do you agree with Lewis—that the only way to understand your need for God is to try to be moral and to fail? Why is the "vital moment" in our lives the moment we give up the struggle?

I clearly recognize that all good is in
God alone, and that in me, without
Divine Grace, there is nothing but
deficiency. . . . The one sole thing in
myself in which I glory, is that I see in
myself nothing in which I can glory.
CATHERINE OF GENOA

To trust Him means, of course, trying to do all that He says. There would be no sense in saying you trusted a person if you would not take his advice. Thus if you have really handed yourself over to Him, it must follow that you are trying to obey Him. But trying in a new way, a less worried way. Not doing these things in order to be saved, but because He has begun to save you already. Not hoping to get to Heaven as a reward for your actions, but inevitably wanting to act in a certain way because a first faint gleam of Heaven is already inside you. —CSL

If you feel loved and secure in a relationship, do you continue to try and earn the other person's love? Or do you do loving things for that person simply because you know you are loved? How does this idea translate into a relationship with God?

Obedience is the
Child of Trust.
JOHN CLIMACUS

I think all Christians would agree with me if I said that though Christianity seems at first to be all about morality, all about duties and rules and guilt and virtue, yet it leads you on, out of all that, into something beyond. One has a glimpse of a country where they do not talk of those things, except perhaps as a joke. Every one there is filled full with what we should call goodness as a mirror is filled with light. But they do not call it goodness. They do not call it anything. They are not thinking of it. They are too busy looking at the source from which it comes. But this is near the stage where the road passes over the rim of our world. No one's eyes can see very far beyond that: lots of people's eyes can see further than mine. —c s l

How does one go from a Christianity that seems to be all about "duties and rules and guilt and virtue" to that "something beyond"? How do you grow out of the constant thought of how to be good and into the constant thought of the One who is good?

They dwell in their own countries but simply as sojourners. . . . They pass their days on earth, but are citizens of heaven. . . . They love all, and are persecuted by all. They are poor, yet they make many rich; they are completely destitute, and yet they enjoy complete abundance. They are reviled, and yet they bless. When they do good they are punished as evildoers; undergoing punishment, they rejoice because they are brought to life.

EPISTLE TO DIOGNETUS
WRITTEN ABOUT 130 A.D.,
ONE OF THE EARLIEST
DESCRIPTIONS OF CHRISTIANS

Study Group Questions for

Christian Behaviour

1. While we all generally agree on the first two parts of morality—being good to others and being good people—there are many opinions on the third part, the overall purpose of life. What do you think is the "general purpose of human life as a whole"?

2. Discuss the "Cardinal virtues"—prudence, temperance, justice, and fortitude. Are they valued in today's society? Why or why not?

3. How can Christian morality be applied to all of the "ordinary human arts and sciences"? What would that look like?

4. What is the role of charity in the world today? How do you perceive the role of charity in the Christian church as a whole?

5. Discuss the idea that we are judged on what we do with our "raw materials" and not on how we seem externally. Does this seem fair or unfair?

6. What are your thoughts on Lewis's view of sexuality, Christian chastity, and the nature of married love?

7. Do you think that you can love your enemies while waging war against them or punishing them?

8. Today's culture does not see pride as a sin, but in many ways sees it as a virtue. In what ways can we still see that pride is destructive?

9. Do you think it's true that you can only come to realize your need for God by trying to be good and failing? Why or why not?

10. The favorite stories and myths of human history speak of other worlds. What do you think this says about reality and human nature? Does it indicate that there is indeed another, better world, as Lewis suggests?

Beyond Personality: Or First Steps in the Doctrine of the Trinity

CHAPTER ONE

Making and Begetting

I remember once when I had been giving a talk to the R.A.F., an old, hard-bitten officer got up and said, 'I've no use for all that stuff. But, mind you, I'm a religious man too. I know there's a God. I've felt Him: out alone in the desert at night: the tremendous mystery. And that's just why I don't believe all your neat little dogmas and formulas about Him. To anyone who's met the real thing they all seem so petty and pedantic and unreal!'

Now in a sense I quite agreed with that man. I think he had probably had a real experience of God in the desert. And when he turned from that experience to the Christian creeds, I think he was really turning from something real to something less real. In the same way, if a man has once looked at the Atlantic from the beach, and then goes and looks at a map of the Atlantic, he also will be turning from something real to something less real: turning from real waves to a bit of coloured paper. But here comes the point. The map is admittedly only coloured paper, but there are two things you have to remember about it. In the first place, it is based on what hundreds and thousands of people have found out by sailing the real Atlantic. In that way it has behind it masses of experience just as real as the one you could have from the beach; only, while yours would be a single glimpse, the map fits all those different experiences together. In the second place, if you want to go anywhere, the map is absolutely necessary. As long as you are content with walks on the beach, your own glimpses are far more fun than looking at a map. But the map is going to be more use than walks on the beach if you want to get to America. —C S L

Why isn't personal experience of God enough? How do theology and experience work together in the Christian life? How are creeds like maps?

None but a theology that came out of eternity can carry you and me safely to and through eternity.
THEODORE LEDYARD CUYLER

But what man, in his natural condition, has not got, is Spiritual life—the higher and different sort of life that exists in God. We use the same word *life* for both: but if you thought that both must therefore be the same sort of thing, that would be thinking that the 'greatness' of space and the 'greatness' of God were the same sort of greatness. In reality, the difference between Biological life and Spiritual life is so important that I am going to give them two distinct names. The Biological sort which comes to us through Nature, and which (like everything else in Nature) is always tending to run down and decay so that it can only be kept up by incessant subsidies from Nature in the form of air, water, food, etc., is *Bios*. The Spiritual life which is in God from all eternity, and which made the whole natural universe, is *Zoe*. *Bios* has, to be sure, a certain shadowy or symbolic resemblance to *Zoe*: but only the sort of resemblance there is between a photo and a place, or a statue and a man. A man who changed from having *Bios* to having *Zoe* would have gone through as big a change as a statue which changed from being a carved stone to being a real man.

And that is precisely what Christianity is about. This world is a great sculptor's shop. We are the statues and there is a rumour going round the shop that some of us are some day going to come to life. —CSL

Have you "come to life"—changed from Bios to Zoe? How are you different? How is your everyday life influenced by this change?

> Since death came through a man, the resurrection of the dead comes also through a man. For as in Adam all die, so in Christ all will be made alive.
>
> 1 CORINTHIANS 15:21–22 NIV

CHAPTER TWO

The Three-Personal God

*T*he human level is a simple and rather empty level. On the human level one person is one being, and any two persons are two separate beings—just as, in two dimensions (say on a flat sheet of paper) one square is one figure, and any two squares are two separate figures. On the Divine level you can still find personalities; but up there you find them combined in new ways which we, who do not live on that level, cannot imagine. In God's dimension, so to speak, you find a being who is three Persons while remaining one Being, just as a cube is six squares while remaining one cube. . . . But we can get a sort of faint notion of it. And when we do, we are then, for the first time in our lives, getting some positive idea, however faint, of something super-personal—something more than a person. It is something we could never have guessed, and yet, once we have been told, one almost feels one ought to have been able to guess it because it fits in so well with all the things we know already. —c s l

What are some things that we "know already" that give us a better understanding of the nature of the Trinity? Like the cube that is six squares but is still a cube, what other real life examples help you with the idea of a "three-Personal God"?

_____

_____

_____

_____

_____

_____

_____

In the unity of the Godhead there be three persons, of one substance, power, and eternity; God the Father, God the Son, and God the Holy Ghost. The Father is of none, neither begotten, nor proceeding: the Son is eternally begotten of the Father: the Holy Ghost eternally proceeding from the Father and the Son.

THE CONFESSION OF FAITH
OF THE WESTMINSTER
ASSEMBLY OF DIVINES, 1646

An ordinary simple Christian kneels down to say his prayers. He is trying to get into touch with God. But if he is a Christian he knows that what is prompting him to pray is also God: God, so to speak, inside him. But he also knows that all his real knowledge of God comes through Christ, the Man who was God—that Christ is standing beside him, helping him to pray, praying for him. You see what is happening. God is the thing to which he is praying—the goal he is trying to reach. God is also the thing inside him which is pushing him on—the motive power. God is also the road or bridge along which he is being pushed to that goal. So that the whole threefold life of the three-personal Being is actually going on in that ordinary little bedroom where an ordinary man is saying his prayers. The man is being caught up into the higher kinds of life—what I call *Zoe* or spiritual life: he is being pulled into God, by God, while still remaining himself. —C S L

———◆———

Does Lewis's explanation give you a better understanding of the nature of the Trinity? How do you experience the working of the three Persons of God in your life?

_____

_____

_____

_____

_____

_____

_____

_____

_____

_____

> Without the Spirit it is not possible to hold the Word of God nor without the Son can any draw near to the Father, for the knowledge of the Father is the Son and the knowledge of the Son of God is through the Holy Spirit.
>
> IRENAEUS

CHAPTER THREE

Time and Beyond Time

Almost certainly God is not in Time. His life does not consist of moments following one another. If a million people are praying to Him at ten-thirty tonight, He need not listen to them all in that one little snippet which we call ten-thirty. Ten-thirty—and every other moment from the beginning of the world—is always the Present for Him. If you like to put it that way, He has all eternity in which to listen to the split second of prayer put up by a pilot as his plane crashes in flames.

That is difficult, I know. Let me try to give something, not the same, but a bit like it. Suppose I am writing a novel. I write 'Mary laid down her work; next moment came a knock at the door!' For Mary who has to live in the imaginary time of my story there is no interval between putting down the work and hearing the knock. But I, who am Mary's maker, do not live in that imaginary time at all. Between writing the first half of that sentence and the second, I might sit down for three hours and think steadily about Mary. I could think about Mary as if she were the only character in the book and for as long as I pleased, and the hours I spent in doing so would not appear in Mary's time (the time inside the story) at all.

This is not a perfect illustration, of course. But it may give just a glimpse of what I believe to be the truth. God is not hurried along in the Time-stream of this universe any more than an author is hurried along in the imaginary time of his own novel. He has infinite attention to spare for each one of us. He does not have to deal with us in the mass. You are as much alone with Him as if you were the only being He had ever created. When Christ died, He died for you individually just as much as if you had been the only man in the world. —CSL

How is your idea of prayer and its importance affected by the thought that God is outside of time?

> The great soul that sits on the throne of the universe is not, never was, and never will be, in a hurry.
> JOSIAH GILBERT HOLLAND

Another difficulty we get if we believe God to be in time is this. Everyone who believes in God at all believes that He knows what you and I are going to do tomorrow. But if He knows I am going to do so-and-so, how can I be free to do otherwise? Well, here once again, the difficulty comes from thinking that God is progressing along the Time-line like us: the only difference being that He can see ahead and we cannot. Well, if that were true, if God *foresaw* our acts, it would be very hard to understand how we could be free not to do them. But suppose God is outside and above the Time-line. In that case, what we call 'tomorrow' is visible to Him in just the same way as what we call 'today'. All the days are 'Now' for Him. He does not remember you doing things yesterday; He simply sees you doing them, because, though you have lost yesterday, He has not. He does not 'foresee' you doing things tomorrow; He simply sees you doing them: because, though tomorrow is not yet there for you, it is for Him. You never supposed that your actions at this moment were any less free because God knows what you are doing. Well, He knows your tomorrow's actions in just the same way—because He is already in tomorrow and can simply watch you. In a sense, He does not know your action till you have done it: but then the moment at which you have done it is already 'Now' for Him. —C S L

What do you think of this idea that God doesn't "foresee" our future, but simply observes our past, present, and future all at the same time? Is this different from what you've always believed about God?

With the Lord a day
is like a thousand
years, and a thousand
years are like a day.
2 PETER 3:8 NIV

CHAPTER FOUR

Good Infection

*T*he whole dance, or drama, or pattern of this three-Personal life is to be played out in each one of us: or (putting it the other way round) each one of us has got to enter that pattern, take his place in that dance. There is no other way to the happiness for which we were made. Good things as well as bad, you know, are caught by a kind of infection. If you want to get warm you must stand near the fire: if you want to be wet you must get into the water. If you want joy, power, peace, eternal life, you must get close to, or even into, the thing that has them. They are not a sort of prize which God could, if He chose, just hand out to anyone. They are a great fountain of energy and beauty spurting up at the very centre of reality. If you are close to it, the spray will wet you: if you are not, you will remain dry. Once a man is united to God, how could he not live forever? Once a man is separated from God, what can he do but wither and die? —C S L

What do you think it means for you to enter the "dance" with God? How does it change how you see life when it is understood as part of what Lewis calls a dramatic "three-Personal life"?

_____

_____

_____

_____

_____

_____

_____

Live near to God, and so all
things will appear to you little in
comparison with eternal realities.
ROBERT MURRAY M'CHEYNE

We are not begotten by God, we are only made by Him: in our natural state we are not sons of God, only (so to speak) statues. We have not got *Zoe* or spiritual life: only *Bios* or biological life which is presently going to run down and die. Now the whole offer which Christianity makes is this: that we can, if we let God have His way, come to share in the life of Christ. If we do, we shall then be sharing a life which was begotten, not made, which always has existed and always will exist. Christ is the Son of God. If we share in this kind of life we also shall be sons of God. We shall love the Father as He does and the Holy Ghost will arise in us. He came into this world and became a man in order to spread to other men the kind of life He has—by what I call 'good infection'. Every Christian is to become a little Christ. The whole purpose of becoming a Christian is simply nothing else. —c s l

Do you agree with Lewis that "the whole purpose of becoming a Christian" is to become like Christ? How does this change how you see your past? How does it change how you see your future?

The whole Christ seeks after each sinner, and when the Lord finds it, he gives himself to that one soul as if he had but that one soul to bless. How my heart admires the concentration of all the Godhead and humanity of Christ in his search after each sheep of his flock.

C. H. SPURGEON

CHAPTER FIVE

The Obstinate Toy Soldiers

The Eternal Being, who knows everything and who created the whole universe, became not only a man but (before that) a baby, and before that a *foetus* inside a Woman's body. If you want to get the hang of it, think how you would like to become a slug or a crab.

The result of this was that you now had one man who really was what all men were intended to be: one man in whom the created life, derived from His Mother, allowed itself to be completely and perfectly turned into the begotten life. The natural human creature in Him was taken up fully into the divine Son. Thus in one instance humanity had, so to speak, arrived: had passed into the life of Christ. And because the whole difficulty for us is that the natural life has to be, in a sense, 'killed', He chose an earthly career which involved the killing of His human desires at every turn—poverty, misunderstanding from His own family, betrayal by one of His intimate friends, being jeered at and manhandled by the Police, and execution by torture. And then, after being thus killed—killed every day in a sense—the human creature in Him, because it was united to the divine Son, came to life again. The Man in Christ rose again: not only the God. That is the whole point. For the first time we saw a real man. One tin soldier—real tin, just like the rest—had come fully and splendidly alive. —C S L

What does it mean to become "fully and splendidly alive"? Using Jesus' life as an example, what does this new life look like?

_____

_____

_____

_____

_____

Salvation is God's way of
making us real people.
AUGUSTINE OF HIPPO

CHAPTER SIX

Two Notes

Christianity thinks of human individuals not as mere members of a group or items in a list, but as organs in a body—different from one another and each contributing what no other could. When you find yourself wanting to turn your children, or pupils, or even your neighbours, into people exactly like yourself, remember that God probably never meant them to be that. You and they are different organs, intended to do different things. On the other hand, when you are tempted not to bother about someone else's troubles because they are 'no business of yours', remember that though he is different from you he is part of the same organism as you. —C S L

Have you ever experienced this everyone-must-have-the-same mentality in the church or in your life? How does it change how we treat others (or how the church treats its members) if we see everyone as different organs in the same body?

If Christ is amongst us, then it is
necessary that we sometimes yield
up our own opinion for the sake of
peace. Who is so wise as to have
perfect knowledge of all things?
Therefore trust not too much to
thine own opinion, but be ready
also to hear the opinions of others.

THOMAS À KEMPIS

CHAPTER SEVEN

Let's Pretend

*I*t is not a question of a good man who died two thousand years ago. It is a living Man, still as much a man as you, and still as much God as He was when he created the world, really coming and interfering with your very self; killing the old natural self in you and replacing it with the kind of self He has. At first, only for moments. Then for longer periods. Finally, if all goes well, turning you permanently into a different sort of thing; into a new little Christ, a being which, in its own small way, has the same kind of life as God; which shares in His power, joy, knowledge and eternity. —CSL

What does it mean for your "old natural self" to be killed? How does this process allow you to share in the life of God? Are you willing to let your natural self be killed?

_____

_____

_____

_____

_____

_____

_____

_____

_____

_____

> The Word introduced Himself into that which He was not, in order that the nature of man also might become what it was not, resplendent, by its union, with the grandeur of divine majesty, which has been raised beyond nature rather than that it has cast the unchangeable God beneath its nature.
>
> CYRIL OF ALEXANDRIA

*I*n a sense you might even say it is God who does the pretending. The three-Personal God, so to speak, sees before Him in fact a self-centered, greedy, grumbling, rebellious human animal. But He says 'Let us pretend that this is not a mere creature, but our Son. It is like Christ in so far as it is a Man, for He became Man. Let us pretend that it is also like Him in Spirit. Let us treat it as if it were what in fact it is not. Let us pretend in order to make the pretence into a reality.' God looks at you as if you were a little Christ: Christ stands beside you to turn you into one. I daresay this idea of a divine make-believe sounds rather strange at first. But, is it so strange really? Is not that how the higher thing always raises the lower? A mother teaches her baby to talk by talking to it as if it understood long before it really does. —C S L

How does God's "pretending" that you are like his Son help you become like Christ in fact? What can you do now to better pretend you are like Jesus?

> Your worthiness gives you no
> help, and your unworthiness
> does not harm you. As one drop
> of water is as compared to the
> great ocean, so are my sins as
> compared with God's
> incomprehensible grace in Christ.
> JOHANN ARNDT

CHAPTER EIGHT

Is Christianity Hard or Easy?

Christ says 'Give me All. I don't want so much of your time and so much of your money and so much of your work: I want You. I have not come to torment your natural self, but to kill it. No half-measures are any good. I don't want to cut off a branch here and a branch there, I want to have the whole tree cut down. I don't want to drill a tooth, or crown it, or stop it, but to have it out. Hand over the whole natural self, all the desires which you think innocent as well as the ones you think wicked—the whole outfit. I will give you a new self instead. In fact, I will give you Myself: my own will shall become yours.'

———— ◆ ————

How do you give your whole self up to God? What seems most threatening about this notion? What is comforting?

_____

_____

_____

_____

_____

_____

_____

_____

_____

_____

_____

> Let us pray God that he would
> root out of our hearts
> everything of our own planting
> and set out there, with his own
> hand, the tree of life bearing all
> manner of fruits.
>
> FRANÇIOS FÉNELON

All your wishes and hopes for the day rush at you like wild animals. And the first job each morning consists simply in shoving them all back; in listening to that other voice, taking that other point of view, letting that other larger, stronger, quieter life come flowing in. And so on, all day. Standing back from all your natural fussings and frettings; coming in out of the wind. —C S L

What do you think this "larger, stronger, quieter life" looks like? How does this "coming in out of the wind" make a practical difference in everyday living?

_____

_____

_____

_____

_____

_____

_____

_____

_____

_____

_____

_____

_____

_____

_____

_____

_____

Be still, and know that I am God.
PSALM 46:10 NIV

What we have been told is how we men can be drawn into Christ—can become part of that wonderful present which the young Prince of the universe wants to offer to His Father—that present which is Himself and therefore us in Him. It is the only thing we were made for. And there are strange, exciting hints in the Bible that when we are drawn in, a great many other things in Nature will begin to come right. The bad dream will be over: it will be morning. —CSL

What is God's purpose is making us like Christ? How might this affect "other things in Nature"?

_____

_____

_____

_____

_____

_____

_____

_____

_____

_____

_____

_____

_____

_____

_____

_____

_____

At the end of the world, when the church of Christ shall be settled in its last, and most complete, and its eternal state . . . divine love shall not fail, but shall be brought to its most glorious perfection in every individual member of the ransomed church above. Then, in every heart, that love which now seems as but a spark, shall be kindled to a bright and glowing flame, and every ransomed soul shall be as it were in a blaze of divine and holy love, and shall remain and grow in this glorious perfection and blessedness through all eternity!

JONATHAN EDWARDS

CHAPTER NINE

Counting the Cost

'Make no mistake,' He says, 'if you let me, I will make you perfect. The moment you put yourself in My hands, that is what you are in for. Nothing less, or other, than that. You have free will, and if you choose, you can push Me away. But if you do not push Me away, understand that I am going to see this job through. Whatever suffering it may cost you in your earthly life, whatever inconceivable purification it may cost you after death, whatever it costs Me, I will never rest, not let you rest, until you are literally perfect—until my Father can say without reservation that He is well pleased with you, as He said He was well pleased with me. This I can do and will do. But I will not do anything less.'

———◆———

Why is it important to God that we be made perfect? What does it really mean to be made perfect?

_____

_____

_____

_____

_____

_____

_____

_____

_____

_____

_____

_____

O Savior, pour upon me thy
Spirit of meekness and love,
Annihilate the selfhood in
me, be thou all my life.
WILLIAM BLAKE

*I*magine yourself as a living house. God comes in to rebuild that house. At first, perhaps, you can understand what He is doing. He is getting the drains right and stopping the leaks in the roof and so on: you knew that those jobs needed doing and so you are not surprised. But presently he starts knocking the house about in a way that hurts abominably and does not seem to make sense. What on earth is He up to? The explanation is that He is building quite a different house from the one you thought of—throwing out a new wing here, putting on an extra floor there, running up towers, making courtyards. You thought you were going to be made into a decent little cottage: but He is building a palace. He intends to come and live in it Himself. —C S L

When have you experienced God's remodeling in your life? What was torn down? What was built up? How are you a different "house" now?

_____

_____

_____

_____

_____

_____

_____

_____

_____

_____

_____

_____

> God wishes to test you like
> gold in the furnace. The
> dross is consumed by the fire,
> but the pure gold remains
> and its value increases.
>
> ST. JEROME EMILIANI

CHAPTER TEN

Nice People or New Men

*I*f you are a nice person—if virtue comes easily to you—beware! Much is expected from those to whom much is given. If you mistake for your own merits what are really God's gifts to you through nature, and if you are contented with simply being nice, you are still a rebel: and all those gifts will only make your fall more terrible, your corruption more complicated, your bad example more disastrous. The Devil was an archangel once; his natural gifts were as far above yours as yours are above those of a chimpanzee.

But if you are a poor creature—poisoned by a wretched upbringing in some house full of vulgar jealousies and senseless quarrels— saddled, by no choice of your own, with some loathsome sexual perversion—nagged day in and day out by an inferiority complex that makes you snap at your best friends—do not despair. He knows all about it. You are one of the poor whom He blessed. He knows what a wretched machine you are trying to drive. Keep on. Do what you can. One day (perhaps in another world, but perhaps far sooner than that) He will fling it on the scrap-heap and give you a new one. And then you may astonish us all—not least yourself: for you have learned your driving in a hard school. (Some of the last will be first and some of the first will be last.) —CSL

Why would it be dangerous to be a "nice person"? Is being aware of your status as a "poor creature" in some ways preferable? What does God want from both the "nice person" and the "poor creature"?

_____

_____

_____

_____

_____

> God is not against us
> because of our sin. He is
> with us against our sin.
> AUTHOR UNKNOWN

CHAPTER ELEVEN

The New Men

Give up yourself, and you will find your real self. Lose your life and you will save it. Submit to death, death of your ambitions and favourite wishes every day and death of your whole body in the end: submit with every fibre of your being, and you will find eternal life. Keep back nothing. Nothing that you have not given away will be really yours. Nothing in you that has not died will ever be raised from the dead. Look for yourself, and you will find in the long run only hatred, loneliness, despair, rage, ruin, and decay. But look for Christ and you will find Him, and with Him everything else thrown in. —C S L

————◆————

What does it mean to "lose your life"? What do you think it looks like to lose yourself, but be found in Christ? How does this change a real life in the real world?

_____

_____

_____

_____

_____

_____

_____

_____

_____

_____

_____

Jesus said, "If anyone would come after me, he must deny himself and take up his cross and follow me. For whoever wants to save his life will lose it, but whoever loses his life for me and for the gospel will save it."

MARK 8:34–35 NIV

Study Group Questions for

BOOK FOUR

Beyond Personality: Or First Steps in the Doctrine of the Trinity

1. Is theology necessary, or is personal experience all that is needed to know God?

2. Discuss Lewis's concept of God as "beyond personal" or "super-personal." How does the theology of the Trinity show us how God is "more than a person"?

3. What does it mean for God to be outside of time? How does this affect the universe as a whole? How does this affect individual people?

4. Discuss the concept of Christianity as an organism. How should we live if we are part of something living, and larger than ourselves? How should we treat others since they are part of this same body with us?

5. How does God perfect us? What does this refining process look like in our everyday lives?

6. While the "killing" of our natural selves sounds painful and difficult, what might be the ultimate benefits? How can we see this principle of death and rebirth in the world around us?